PLOTTO
Instruction Booklet

Master the Plotto System in Seven Lessons

by William Wallace Cook

Suitable for use with

Plotto: The Master Book of All Plots

*Plotto: The Classic Plot Suggestion Tool
for Writers of Creative Fiction*

*Plotto: A New Method of Plot Suggestion
for Writers of Creative Fiction*

Norton Creek Press
http://www.nortoncreekpress.com

Plotto Instruction Booklet
Master the Plotto System in Seven Lessons

by William Wallace Cook
Foreword by Robert Plamondon

ISBN 978-1-938099-04-5

Foreword

This *Plotto Instruction Booklet* has been out of print since 1934, which is a shame, since it's difficult to figure out how to use *Plotto* without it!

Originally used by William Wallace Cook as the textbook for a course in using *Plotto,* it goes through both the mechanics and the philosophy of creating plots with *Plotto*.

The *Plotto Instruction Booklet* in its original form is almost impossible to find, and in fact I owned a copy of *Plotto* for years before even realized that it existed. I was fortunate enough to track down a copy only 60 miles away and borrow it long enough to copy it. The result, reformatted and lightly edited, is what you're reading now.

Plotto is the opposite of a random plot generator: using it will not write a story for you, or even structure one. It offers suggestions that you are expect to—required to—customize to fit the needs of your story. Plotto is a structured way of stimulating your imagination into creating the situations and conflicts you need, whether for a short story, a screenplay, or a novel.

A century ago, William Wallace Cook was a pulp fiction writer famous for his immense output, solid creativity, and his use of organization and technology to ease the task of writing stories at high speed. His non-fiction books, *Plotto* and The *Fiction Factory,* are available through Norton Creek Press.

Happy plotting!

Robert Plamondon

Contents

1. Plotto Masterplots 5

2. Plotto Purposes and Obstacles 14

3. Originality in the Interpretation of Conflict Suggestions 24

4. The Conflict References 31

5. Original Conflict References 38

6. Characterization 46

7. Individualizing Plotto 52

1. Plotto Masterplots

Read and study this manual. It will teach you how to understand and get the most benefit out of Plotto.

> *Remember: Plotto is the greatest single aid in plotting ever offered writers. Make up your mind NOW to give Plotto and this manual the time it deserves. The best-known writers in the world own and use Plotto.*

You are beginning the study of one of the most fascinating problems to be found in any profession. The problem deals with complications of incidents based on human reactions to the various stimuli of environment, each complication unfolding logically into a climax, or crisis, and then subsiding quickly in a denouement. To solve this problem crudely is one thing, but to accomplish it with an art in which the imagination exercises taste and discrimination is quite another thing.

In this life, there is no pleasure and no satisfaction to be compared with the act of *Creating,* or drawing upon our experience for the purpose of giving to the world something *new*, shaped out of materials as old as Man and quickened to life by the breath of the imagination. The artist may do this with a picture, the sculptor with a statue, or the writer with a fictional story—if it chance that each and all of them shall bring originality to bear upon the work.

There can be no hard and fast rules for Genius, and there are only a few simple guideposts that mark the path of Originality; and these guideposts merely exercise and develop the imagination on the progress toward the goal. As Memory is nothing more than the association of ideas, so Originality is nothing more than the combining of those ideas in conformity with an individual conception.

Each person that lives, has ever lived or shall live is, was or will be a collector of ideas combined into a certain thing called experience. My experience is not your experience; and that means that neither you nor I, when accomplishing original work, will accomplish identical work. If it were otherwise, there would be no originality in the world. Originality is our response to the stimulus of *suggestion* in individual terms of our varying experience.

Plotto is a new method of plot *Suggestion* for writers of *Creative* fiction. Let us, here at the beginning of our course, place the emphasis on the word *Suggestion*, as well as on that other word, *Creative*. In later lessons of the course we shall go more deeply into this matter of the interpretation of suggestion. For the present, however, it is merely necessary to note that the interpretation of suggestion results in creative work only when the constructive imagination builds with material hewn from the quarry of individual experience. In other words, we achieve Originality; and Originality is the ideal of the Plotto method of plot construction through the interpretation of plot suggestion.

The Theme

Every story, long or short, grave or gay, mystery story, detective story, love story, or what-not has one basic element in common; and that basic element is the Theme. A Theme is a general proposition defining the story's type. "A man's revenge for the treachery of a false friend," is vaguely descriptive of a certain type of story. "Love in conflict with duty," would be another Theme. Fannie Hurst's powerful story, "She Walks in Beauty," might have for its Theme, "The secret of a mother's tragic weakness kept inviolate through the devotion and sacrifice of a daughter." Frank Luther Mott's strong story, "The Man with a Good Face," might exemplify the Theme, "How the search for good uplifts and ennobles the Seeker."

Themes are so general in their definition that any number of distinctly different stories may be written to conform to each one. "The Scarlet Letter," by Nathaniel Hawthorne, and "The Silence of Dean Maitland," by Maxwell Gray (Mrs. Craigie) are vastly different as finished stories, although they embody a common Theme.

When a Theme Becomes a Masterplot

Plotto resolves the Theme into a general proposition involving the protagonist, the circumstances the protagonist is called upon to meet, and the outcome of the conflict between the protagonist's purpose and the obstacle or obstacles it encounters. The Theme thus sets a pattern for the situations it comprehends, and so becomes a Masterplot. In Plotto, the Clauses of the Masterplot are interchangeable, thus making it possible to evolve a Masterplot for any story that has ever been written, or that can be written. By reason of the interchangeable Clauses, thousands of Masterplots are made available, and each Masterplot may be the source of thousands of distinctly different stories.

Kindly turn to the Masterplot Chart, beginning at page eleven in the Plotto book.

Interchangeable Masterplot Clauses

Note, please, that each Masterplot consists of three Clauses, an "A" Clause, a "B" Clause and "C" Clause. Those three Clauses carry the plot technically from its introduction, through ascending action to crisis and on to denouement. The A Clause is the protagonist clause, the B Clause initiates and carries on the action, and the C Clause carries on and terminates the action.

Thus No. 1 of the A Clause, No. 1 of the B Clause and No. 1 of the C Clause, read consecutively, give the Masterplot: "A person in love, engaging in a difficult enterprise when promised a reward for high achievement, pays a grim penalty in an unfortunate undertaking." From this, Victor Hugo might have written his "Toilers of the Sea," and from it, also, any number of writers could write any number of stories, all unlike, and yet all conforming to this general proposition. This Masterplot has an unhappy ending, very powerful as Hugo's master imagination deals with it; but the unhappy ending may be changed by selecting another terminal, or C Clause. "Emerges happily from a serious entanglement," would be one change, "Achieves success and happiness in a hard undertaking" would be another, or "Rescues integrity from a serious entanglement" would be still another.

The A Clause indicates in a general way the character or the status of the protagonist.

The protagonist of A Clause No. 1 is defined as "A Person in Love." This merely defines the status of the protagonist, whose character would develop from the situations, or whose character would develop the situations. The name of this particular character is legion. Such a protagonist brought about the siege of Troy, with all its mighty convulsions shaking earth and moving heaven.

Here in this Chart, as everywhere else in Plotto, the Clauses merely suggest. And this protagonist may have been "in love" at the beginning of the B Clause action, or the sentiment of love may develop as the B Clause action develops. The banal truth remains that there can be no love story unless there is a "person in love." A person may pretend to be in love, but such a person would fall into the A Clause No. 11 category, "A Person Swayed by Pretense."

Every story in which some phase of married life is the dominant Theme will have A Clause No. 2 for its protagonist, another Clause which defines the status of the leading character—"A Married Person." Here again the name of the protagonist is legion.

The character of the person playing the stellar role is suggested in A Clause No. 3, "A Lawless Person." If the doubtful experiment is tried of having a criminal for a hero, a sort of "Raffles," or "Wallingford," this A Clause would serve. It would also define a protagonist who rebels against less serious conventions and is the exemplar of his or her own sweet will.

"An Erring Person," protagonist of Masterplot No. 4, may be erring in any manner suggested by the imagination, morally, legally, in judgment or otherwise.

"Benevolent Person" may be a philanthropist, or a kindly soul whose care and consideration have nothing to do with money, but with service. "A Protecting Person" is one who seeks to save another from threatening misfortune in all the many ways which our complicated system of living make possible. "A Person of Ideals" may be a person of false ideals, of criminal ideals or of worthy ideals. "A Person Influenced by an Obligation" may be influenced by an obligation of his own, or by the obligation of another. "A Person Subjected to Adverse Conditions" is a protagonist who is facing some sort of misfortune, or what he considers misfortune. "A Resentful Person" is a protagonist who sounds any or all the deeps of revenge. "A Person Swayed by Pretense," may be swayed by his own pretense, or the pretense of another. "A Subtle Person" may be subtle in good or evil methods, in admirable ways or in ways that are pernicious. "A person Influenced by the Occult and the Mysterious" could be a Cagliostro, or the victim of a Cagliostro. "A Normal Person" may be a protagonist whom the world considers normal, although that does not obscure his individuality. We all have our own dispositions, and the normal person does not depart so widely from the traits or conventions as to place himself in any of the other A Clauses already enumerated. He might be normal throughout most of the action, and become abnormal in the C Clause.

A Clause No. 15 is the first Clause of the indefinite Masterplot. If any protagonist can be devised that is out of harmony with any of the other A Clauses, here is the place for that character.

You will note that the Clauses are so constructed that they will serve for either a <u>male</u> or a <u>female</u> protagonist. In that respect, they are impersonal.

The propositions shadowed forth by the B Clauses are self-explanatory; and so, also, are the vague definitions of the C Clauses.

The question may be asked: "Well, what about those thousands of Masterplots? They are not plots." No, they are not plots.

> *A Masterplot is not a plot; a plot calls for detailed suggestions, and the Masterplot merely suggests the Theme and provides a string upon which to thread the situations exemplifying it.*

By approaching the plot through a Masterplot, however, we define the story's limits and provide a basis for the situations it embodies. The general suggestions of the Masterplots, as you will discover later on, lead us to concrete suggestions for cutting the cloth of situation to correspond with a pattern Theme.

Kindly observe that there are <u>fifteen</u> A Clauses and fifteen C Clauses but <u>sixty-two</u> B Clauses; and that all the Clauses are interchangeable, so that any A Clause may be used in juxtaposition with any B Clause, and with any C Clause. Each of the A Clauses has sixty-two variations when used in connection with the B Clauses, and each of the sixty-two variations has fifteen more variations when running the gamut of the C Clauses.

Masterplots: Simple and Compound

For practical story-writing purposes we may consider Plotto Masterplots either as Simple or Compound.

A Simple Masterplot will consist of one A, one B and one C Clause. A Compound Masterplot will consist of combinations of A, B and C Clauses—combinations of all the Clauses or of any one of the Clauses; all combinations in A to be formed of A Clauses, in B of B Clauses and in C of C Clauses.

Only the advanced plottoist should attempt the use of Compound Masterplots, since they involve a complexity of Conflict suggestions with which only the trained imagination may deal to the best advantage. Nevertheless, it is well that the beginner in the Plotto Method should have some knowledge of the manner in which the Masterplot Clauses may be amplified.

Compounding the Masterplot Clauses

The A Clauses, for illustration, might be combined in a single Masterplot, thus: "(1) A Person in Love, (7) A Person of Ideals..." Here the status as well as the character of the, protagonist will be defined in general terms. Again: "(1) A Person in Love, (7) A Person of Ideals, (8) Influenced by the Occult and the Mysterious..." "(3) A Lawless Person, (4) Erring and (11) Swayed by Pretense..." "(1) A Person in Love. (14) A Normal Person, (4) Erring and (10) Resentful..."

The character, or the status and the character, of the protagonist will depend upon the action suggested by the B Clauses. B Clause Combinations may be illustrated as follows:

"(1) engaging in a difficult enterprise when promised a reward for high achievement, and (43) seeking to overcome personal limitations in carrying out an enterprise..." "(38) Committing a grievous mistake and seeking in secret to live down its evil results, and (39) forsaking cherished ambitions to carry out an obligation, and (34) embarking upon an enterprise of insurrection in the hope of ameliorating certain evil conditions..." "(50) Being impelled by an unusual motive to engage in crafty enterprise, and (48) assuming the character of a criminal in a perfectly honest enterprise, and (22) following a wrong course through mistaken judgment..."

The C Clauses in a similar manner may be compounded, as: "(7) Reverses certain opinions when their fallacy is revealed, and (9) achieve success and happiness in a hard undertaking." "(12) Rescues integrity from a serious entanglement, and (8) achieves a spiritual victory."

Beginning With a Masterplot

Rarely perhaps does a writer begin a story with a set Theme before him. He is more likely to begin with a striking situation, and develop the situation forward and backward until presently, consciously or unconsciously, he *feels* the Theme and marshals his situations to its pattern. Now, with the Plotto Masterplot Chart, we may begin with a Masterplot and select our situations to correspond with it. For the present, this is considered the most practical means for gaining a comprehensive working knowledge of the Plotto Method.

A Masterplot selected from Plotto will suggest, vaguely perhaps, the situations to be used in writing a story around it. From an identical suggestion, however, no two of you could write a story that would be at all similar,—except as to Theme. Drawing on your own experience for situations, and for circumstances explanatory of the situations, all stories from an identical Masterplot would be *original* and *different*.

Lesson 1 Exercises

1. What A Clause would you suggest for the protagonist of the old story of "Robinson Crusoe?"
2. What B Clause would you suggest for the same story?
3. What C Clause would you suggest for the same story?
4. What A, B and C Clauses would you suggest for the Bible story, "The Prodigal Son?"
5. Read any short story in current fiction and resolve it into its Masterplot.
    a. Name of Story.
    b. The Masterplot.
6. Invent a Masterplot of your own for the indefinite Masterplot No. 15.
    a. The A Clause.
    b. The B Clause
    c. The C Clause.
7. What B Clause of the Masterplots appeals most powerfully to you?

2. Plotto Purposes and Obstacles

Purpose Rooted in Desire

Desire, in some one of its many forms, is responsible for the awakening of Purpose. A friend of yours has a new automobile. You note how much better his car is than your own. You feel that you would like to have a car of the same make. This feeling grows until you propose to yourself that you will have a car like this new one of your friend's. Here we have a commonplace case of desire begetting Purpose.

Purpose Confronts an Obstacle

Let us further suppose, however, that you have no ready money with which to buy your new car. You are in debt, let us say, and have so many pressing obligations that you feel it is going to be very difficult to finance the purchase of the new car. You could "turn in" the old car and go into debt for the balance of the purchase money needed for the new car. But you are averse to piling up any more debts. Very likely in your financial condition you should not buy the new car at all; nevertheless, desire is so strong that it will not allow you to give over your Purpose. A situation develops in which Purpose is confronted by an Obstacle. The Purpose is to buy a new car, and the Obstacle is lack of ready funds. You cast about for some way in which you can overcome the Obstacle.

Obstacle Apparently Overcome

It happens, we will imagine, that you have owned a lot in a city suburb for a long time. The suburb, for one reason or another, is not growing, lot values are stationary and sales of property hard to encompass. Suddenly, as you are wondering how you are to finance the deal for the new car, you have an offer for your suburban lot. On the strength of this offer, you turn in your old car and sign a contract for the new one to be delivered a short time later.

So far, the situation has not developed anything dramatic. You overcome your Obstacle through the chance offer for your lot.

Obstacle Becomes Formidable

Suppose now your new car is to be delivered on a certain day; and on that day you are to pay in cash the difference in value between your old car and the new one. Let us imagine that the prospective purchaser of your lot dies suddenly, or experiences a pecuniary loss which makes it impossible for him to buy your lot. You are at your wits' end to know what to do, and the situation becomes dramatic because your Obstacle, which you supposed had been overcome, has not been overcome. You are so hard-pressed for funds that you cannot even purchase the new car on comparatively small monthly payments—and you have already contracted with the dealer to take over the new car and pay cash for it on delivery. Your situation becomes desperate. Your Obstacle, so far from having been overcome, is now more formidable than it was at first. What are you going to do? Overcome the Obstacle, or let it overcome you?

The Conflict that Makes a Story

This, as an illustration of Purpose and Obstacle in Conflict, is of the common or garden variety; nevertheless, it emphasizes the fact that there would have been no dramatic situation if your Purpose had not encountered an Obstacle that has become most formidable.

    A little reflection will convince you that there can be no dramatic story situation unless Purpose encounters Obstacles. The resulting Conflict makes the story.

Drama

From the hour of our birth on this planet our Purpose is *to Live*. The Obstacle every life encounters is *Death*. As Schopenhauer puts it, "The Will is a will to live; and its eternal enemy is death." Some of our Purposes during life may be to achieve wealth, or fame, or marriage with the woman of our choice. Obstacles that might defeat these Purposes or might be forced to yield to them, are infinite in number. Whether we win or lose, or whether the result is a "draw," the Conflict gives us our situations. And the Conflict gives us *Drama* if the situations are tense enough.

Suspense

Suspense hangs upon the breathless Conflict between Purpose and Obstacle. Is the protagonist to conquer, or be conquered? We mark his efforts at every stage of the fight; as the Purpose grows in intensity, winning here, losing there, and everything is growing doubt, the suspense becomes acute. Then we have the climax, or crisis, in which the question is to be decided finally one way or the other. The victory is with, or against, the protagonist. The battle ends, and suspense ends with it.

Happiness the Supreme Purpose

The Supreme Purpose of life in "this best of all possible worlds" is to *achieve* Happiness. Happiness, for the late James G. Blaine, the eminent statesman, lay in accomplishing his desire to become President of the United States. Almost overnight an Obstacle developed and shattered his hopes. Happiness for the late Woodrow Wilson lay in winning our country to the League of Nations. The Obstacle that shattered that dream was an Obstacle that could not be overcome. A prospect of happiness breeds desire, and desire is the father of Purpose.

But happiness has not the same meaning for all of us. A certain protagonist of Guy de Maupessant's saw happiness in winning the Cross of the Legion of Honor. There is a doubtful happiness in successful crime, a doubtful happiness in revenge, a noble happiness in self-sacrifice, a worthy happiness in being honest in the face of great temptation to be dishonest. The character of the protagonist indicates for him the meaning of the word "happiness."

Subordinate Purposes

Subordinate Purposes group themselves about the pursuit of happiness. With the Supreme Obstacle of Death threatening us all, we wage our mimic wars of conquest and of gain. The happiness of wealth, of fame, of success in love, of writing a great story, of winning the Distinguished Service Medal, is a happiness subordinate to the main Purpose, *to Live;* and all life is under threat of life's Supreme Obstacle. And so we strive in The Great Shadow, eagerly competing with each other in the pursuit of happiness.

Plotto's Axiom

Plotto lays down few rules. Plotto merely suggests, does away with rules and asks you to follow the bent of your own individual imagination, rightly controlled. But if Plotto might enunciate an axiom, it would be this:

Purpose (expressed or implied) opposing Obstacle (expressed or implied) yields Conflict.

Conflict is the source of suspense, and suspense is the magnet of our interest in all Conflicts.

When Robinson Crusoe finds tracks in the sand, Conflict is dimly foreshadowed and suspense begins. When the mortgage is almost due to the Old Homestead, and the only hope is the success of the horse "Cold Molasses" in the race, we have suspense. When the hero of "Blue Jeans" is roped to the log in the sawmill and the log started toward the roaring buzz saw, the suspense becomes agonizing. When the Prodigal Son leaves the husks and the swine to return to his father, we have suspense. While the Conflict grows, suspense grows; when the suspense is over, the story is done.

Purposes and Obstacles are rift in the B Clauses of the Masterplot; and the B Clauses are illustrated with Conflict suggestions for exemplifying them.

Plan of the Plotto Lessons

There are many angles to Plotto which will be discussed and explained in these lessons. The Plotto book, as you have it, is the result of years of study and research on the part of its author. An endeavor is being made in the lessons to approach the Plotto Method of Plot suggestion systematically, and in a way that will facilitate your use of the book. The lessons have been planned with the idea of taking the various steps toward a complete understanding of Plotto in an orderly manner.

Plotto "Suggests"

You would be surprised to learn how some very knowing people have misunderstood Plotto. On glancing at it, some of the intelligentsia have jumped at the false conclusion that Plotto is a dictionary of situations, a mechanism that yields a cut-and-dried plot by the mere use of a thumb index. Plotto, to the contrary, merely suggests the situations for the plot, explains what is to be done through Purpose and Obstacle, and even offers further suggestions as to the way in which it should be done.

The Conflicts are suggestions, in the form of Purpose and Obstacle, for exemplifying the action suggested by the Masterplot. If you will turn to Conflict 6a, you will find the following:

Conflict 6a

> A, traveling the highroad, drops a purse of money unnoticed *B, who has long desired to know A, picks up the purse he has dropped and returns it. A and B fall in love**

If we have A for our protagonist, his Purpose will be to find the purse he has lost. His Obstacle will be the long stretch of road he has covered before discovering his loss, and the chance that some one else has found and kept the purse.

With B as the protagonist, her Purpose will be to make the acquaintance of A. The Obstacle is the fact that they are strangers to each other, and that they have no mutual friend who can bring them together. The Obstacle is overcome when B finds and returns the purse. As a result of their later association, A and B fall in love.

A, on his part, knows that he will be happier if he can find his purse; and B, on her part, feels that she will be happier if she can make the acquaintance of A. For A, as it is for B, happiness will be won if their romance ends in marriage. A's Purpose is now to win B in marriage. What is the Obstacle? Let us for illustration, turn to another Conflict.

Conflict 54a

> A is in love with B. One evening, as usual, he calls to see B; but, where her beautiful home had stood, no later than the evening before, there is now only an ancient, time-stained tomb—the tomb of B, who had died a hundred years before A was born.

Here we are plunged into the occult and the supernatural. A's Purpose to marry B has met an Obstacle of a mysterious nature which it is impossible for him to overcome. C Clause (13) of the Masterplot would apply here: "Comes finally to the blank wall of enigma." The resulting story, based on such a plot, would go Rider Haggard's "She" one better.

Let us still, for purposes of illustration, look at another Conflict.

Conflict 153

> A, in love with B, has a valuable gift sent to B by a jeweler* Through error, or by evil intent, packages are transposed; and the gift received by B, as from A, very nearly proves disastrous to A's love affair**

A's Purpose, naturally, is to please B and so forward his love affair. The Obstacle the Purpose encounters is the transposition of packages.

Conflict 432a

> A, married to B, seeks by secret enterprise to effect a change in unpleasant matrimonial conditions.

What is the Purpose here? It is plainly expressed. What is the Obstacle? It is implied, and it is indefinite. It will be expressed plainly enough when the abstract suggestion, "unpleasant matrimonial conditions," is resolved into something concrete.

Interpreting Purpose and Obstacle

It is not the purpose in this lesson to intrude upon the interpretation of Conflict suggestion, for that is a comprehensive matter to be considered in later lessons. We wish now merely to make it possible for each student to understand how to arrive at a determination of the Purpose and Obstacle in each Conflict.

Conflict 754

>A gambles with money he is holding in trust.

This is a short Conflict. The Purpose is implied and also the Obstacle. A seeks gain by gambling. He has no money of his own, and that is his Obstacle. An acute need for money leads to the desire that inspires his Purpose. He overcomes his Obstacle by committing an error, perhaps a crime; that is, he gambles with money he is holding in trust.

It is very important that this lesson be thoroughly mastered; and that in addition to answering the questions of the Work Sheet, the student take time to dip into the Plotto Conflicts at random and exercise the imagination by resolving the Conflicts into their Purposes and Obstacles.

Lesson 2 Exercises

1. Note the latter half of Conflict 10a; "B, a criminal arrested by A, a detective, brings her charms to bear upon A in the hope of affecting her escape."

a. What is B's Purpose?

   b. What is A's Purpose?

   c. What is B's Obstacle?

   d. How would you interpret A's implied Obstacle?

2. Note Conflict 561: "A, husband of B, receives anonymous communications regarding B and A-3."

   a. Interpret A's Implied Purpose?

   b. Interpret A's Implied Obstacle?

3. Consider the second half of Conflict 681b: "A recovers from a critical illness but loses all remembrance of his personal identity."

   a. Interpret an implied Purpose for A.

   b. Interpret the Obstacle.

4. Conflict 834: "A, becoming secretly aware of the plans for a holdup, endeavors to prevent it."

   a. A's Purpose?

   b. Interpret A's Implied Obstacle.

5. Conflict 1403: "A secures knowledge of an important secret, and his curiosity involves him in a queer enterprise."

   a. What is A's Implied Purpose?

   b. Interpret an Implied Obstacle.

6. You were asked, in the First Lesson Work Sheet, to select from the Masterplots of the Masterplot Chart, a Masterplot that carried a particular appeal to you. You are now requested to select a Conflict exemplifying the B Clause of your Masterplot, a Conflict that appeals to you. You will do this by turning to Page 16 in Plotto, finding there the number of B Clause of your Masterplot, and then turning to the sub-group of Conflicts that suggest a situation. Or, if you desire, you may run through all the Plotto Conflicts and

select one which, you think, will exemplify the particular B Clause. Write out that Conflict in its entirety, being sure to prefix its number.

3. Originality in the Interpretation of Conflict Suggestions

One of the most important words in any language is *Experience*.

The immortal Patrick Henry "had but one lamp by which his feet were guided, and that was the lamp of Experience." Richter was speaking of Experience when he said: "The youngest heart has the same waves within it as the oldest, but without the plummet which can measure their depths." Had Spurgeon been writing of Plotto he could not have enunciated a more pertinent truth than this: "Conflicts bring experience; and experience brings that growth in grace which is not to be obtained by any other means." William Matthews has his to say about Experience: "The petty cares, the minute anxieties, the infinite littles which go to make up the sum of human experience, like the invisible granules of powder, give the last and highest polish to a character." And there is this by John Locke: "Experience: in that all our knowledge is founded; and from that it ultimately derives itself. Our observation employed either about external or sensible objects or about the internal operations of our own minds, perceived and reflected on by ourselves, is that which supplies our understandings with all the materials of thinking."

From this brief symposium we may safely gather that Experience is an individual's fund of knowledge; or, as Hosea Ballou writes: "Experience is retrospect knowledge." Our contact with our fellows, and with the physical world, gives us our experience; and reflection upon such contacts, or the lessons derived from them, becomes the spiritual part of our fund of knowledge."

Individual Experiences Never Identical

It is impossible that this world should contain two persons of mature years whose fund of knowledge is exactly the same. As human beings differ in nature and in temperament, so the lessons they draw from Experience will vary. If it were possible for your Experience and my Experience to be identical, nevertheless the deductions drawn from those Experiences would widely differentiate our fund of garnered knowledge. We are individuals, and we individualize our findings. In that we all of us are Original.

Originality

Originality, therefore, means the interpretation of suggestion each according to his own Experience. The interpretation is not copied, imitated or translated, but it is new and genuine. It is inventive, also, and suggestive of new thoughts and combinations.

Let us consider a part of Conflict 618: "A is bored by certain duties he is obliged to perform." Turn that suggestion over in your mind. Give yourself three minutes to reach down into your own Experience and interpret the duties which A is obliged to perform, and which bore him.

Interpretation by Different Persons Not Identical

It must be clear to all of you, from this little demonstration, that Conflict suggestions cannot be interpreted in identical terms if these interpretations are original—that is, based on individual Experience. Now, again, let us take the second part of Conflict 618: "A, bored by certain duties he is obliged to perform, finds a way out—with unpleasant results." Using your interpretation of the first suggestion as a basis, endeavor to interpret this second suggestion in original terms. You may have five minutes for this.

Originality in the Interpretation of Specific Conflicts

Another angle of Conflict suggestion is exemplified by Conflict 617, just above 618 in the Plotto Conflicts: "A shows his ignorance of the usages of high society by unpacking his satchel when a servant, A-7, is expected to do it for him. A, annoyed by a *faux pas* he has committed, seeks to 'save his face.'

You will not actually use the satchel incident. This is a Specific, rather than a General Conflict, and A's unpacking of the satchel is cited merely as an illustration. You will not be original if you make use of the satchel in interpreting the suggestion. What other *faux pas* could A commit? Perhaps some of you may have had an Experience of your own, or have witnessed, or have heard of some incident in which a person unused to the customs of "high society" committed a breach of etiquette, or transgressed the conventions. Fit that incident in here. Perhaps there are a few who will remember how, in "Joshua Whitcomb," the rural protagonist found himself in a luxurious city home—an environment with which he was not familiar—looked around for a cuspidor, failed to find one, and thereupon took an expensive vase from the mantel and stood it beside his chair.

Originality the Soul of Creative Art

All this may seem very simple to some of you, but nevertheless it is training your imagination along inventive lines. You are drilling yourself in the art of explaining circumstances in original terms. Not alone in story writing, but in every field of human endeavor, the highest success comes to those with an imagination highly developed and rightly controlled; that is, with an imagination that exercises taste and discrimination in dealing with suggestion. And note, please, that discrimination includes good judgment. Remember that Originality is the Soul of Creative Art, and to become a writer of truly creative fiction you must develop a facility in applying Originality to your plot construction.

Studies in Interpretation

Let us study for a moment the first part of broken Conflict 1136: "B sends a telegram to her maid, B-7, to 'come at once.'" There is a veiled suggestion in this part of the Conflict. Reduce the Conflict to a Purpose. B needs the services of her maid. Where is the maid? Possibly away on a vacation. Why does B need the maid? A sudden and imperative summons compels B to take a journey, and she cannot travel without her maid.

These are but two of many interpretations of the suggestion. The latter half of the Conflict suggests the Obstacle: "B, intending to send a telegram to her maid, B-7, through error addresses the message to A." Thus we have a situation. How could B fall into such an error? Presumably because A is very much in her mind—so much in her mind that unconsciously she addresses her telegram to A instead of to B-7. What is there between A and B which would make such a message as B has sent of vital moment? What circumstances would make the situation interesting? A might be a discarded lover, a worthy lover discarded through a misunderstanding. A might be a man with whom B has quarreled over a matter in which B is wholly in the wrong. Your Experience would suggest an interpretation of the suggestion which my own Experience would not indicate to me.

Glance for a moment at the first half of Conflict 1350: "A thinks himself obsessed with a fear of speeding automobiles." A's Purpose is implied: He thinks himself obsessed with a fear; and his implied Purpose is to free himself of that fear. Now note the Obstacle developed in the second half of the Conflict: "A, in order to disprove a fancied hallucination, deliberately throws himself in front of a speeding automobile which he supposes to be a phantom."

Original interpretation of this suggestion will eliminate automobiles altogether. A might think himself obsessed with a fear of burglars. The suggestion of the complete Conflict is this: In order to cure himself of a fancied obsession, A faces a real burglar who is looting his home; and he supposes the burglar to be a phantom until—But we pause here, as we are getting into other circumstances which other Conflict suggestions will embody.

A might be a hunter in a wilderness, looking for deer. He might be obsessed with the fear that he will shoot another hunter by mistake. He sees a flash of white through the trees and undergrowth; in order to conquer his supposed obsession, he aims his rifle and shoots at something that is not a deer, and—Again we are at the end of Conflict 1350, and we pause to carry on with another situation.

A might be obsessed with the fear that he will be killed by a falling wall. In order to overcome his fancied obsession, he breaks through the fire lines near a burning building, and a wall topples.

We have gone a long way from speeding automobiles. Many interpretations of this suggestion will occur to you which could not possibly occur to me, since the fund of Experience upon which we draw is different.

When B, in the other Conflict, sends a telegram to her maid to "Come at once," the wording of the message itself is only a suggestion. The text of the telegram could be altered as your original interpretation of the suggestion might demand. So, also, the text of the later conflict suggestion might be altered in any manner that occurs to your groping imagination. Whatever the suggestion suggests to your Experience, make the most of it.

Working Originally

When writing a story, you will invent circumstances in interpreting a suggestion, and these circumstances will be original with you, and the story will flow easily along familiar lines of Experience. We work Originally, and we work best, with materials of our own. The suggestion alone is Plotto's; the working out of the suggestion is original with you and is yours alone.

No Hard and Fast Rules

A Conflict suggestion carries with it no hard and fast rules of procedure. Suggestions from the Plotto Conflict set the imagination at work along lines germane to the story plot, and so long as the situation is exemplified the circumstances used in exemplifying it will make no change in the general trend of the B Clause of the Masterplot. The interpretation in many cases will depart widely from the Specific Conflict's concrete illustration; and that will be admirable, so long as the suggestion is bodied forth in your original interpretation. The interpretation of the suggestion may carry you far from the Conflict with which you are working; that will be well, too, for the suggestion has set your mind to working along new lines.

Lesson 3 Exercises

1. Conflict 705: "A, unable to conquer his misfortunes, seeks to escape them by committing suicide."
   a. Name three misfortunes which might bring A to such a desperate pass.
2. Conflict 588: "B, dying, reveals to her husband, A, a closely guarded secret which he finds greatly perturbing."
   a. What was the secret B revealed to A? Name three secrets she might have revealed.
3. Conflict 206: "A, in love with B, discovers that his rival, A-3, is unworthy, B seems to favor A-3."
   a. In what way is A-3 unworthy?
   b. Why does B *seem* to favor A-3?
4. Conflict 1410: "A, endeavoring to solve a mystery, has for his only clue, X, the portrait of a beautiful woman painted on ivory."
   a. What mystery is A endeavoring to solve?
   b. What other clue could there be besides the portrait?
   c. How did the clue fall into A's hands?
   d. What is A's reason for endeavoring to solve the mystery?
   e. Give another reason for A's attempting to solve the mystery
5. What was the B Clause of the Masterplot you selected?
   a. What Conflict did you select to exemplify this B Clause?
   b. Give an original interpretation of that Conflict.

4. The Conflict References

With this lesson we shall begin considering another angle of this method of Conflict suggestion.

You have noticed in the Conflicts that, in lieu of proper names, Plotto makes use of letter symbols, or of letters and numerals. These symbols represent the characters, the dramatis personae, of the Conflicts; they suggest, also, the relationship of subordinate characters to the protagonist, or the action suggested by the Conflict. As an illustration: "Tom seeks to help Dick in a certain enterprise.* Tom, seeking to help Dick in a certain enterprise, does not know that Dick is a crook.**" Instead of using the names "Tom" and "Dick" Plotto's Conflict 809 would phase the Purpose and Obstacle in this way: "A seeks to help A-5 in a certain enterprise.* A, seeking to help A-5 in a certain enterprise, does not know that A-5 is a crook.**"

Now, the use of "A" and "A-5" instead of the proper names, "Tom" and "Dick," offers several practical advantages. We know at once that A is the leading character, the protagonist; and we know A-5 is a male criminal. Wherever a criminal appears in the Conflicts, the added figure, 5, will indicate it.

The Symbols

So the symbols make for a certain uniformity in suggesting the characters taking part in the Conflict. They have also, as previously stated, the additional value of expressing the relationship of subordinate characters to the protagonist, or to the action.

The use of these symbols, also, is a very practical aid in Conflict manipulations, since they may be readily changed, or transposed, to meet the varying needs of the moment.

The more intimate relationships, consanguineous or by marriage, have letter symbols. "F-A," for example, is "The father of A," "SN-A" is the "son of A," and "M-B" is the "mother of B."

It is merely necessary for the plottoist to remember that "A" is the male protagonist, and the female protagonist is always "B." Other relationships than ties of blood or marriage are indicated by the use of numerals. Thus, "A-2" is a "friend of A," and "B-2" is a "friend of B," the "A" suggesting a man friend and the "B" a woman friend; and "bA-2," if desired, would suggest a woman friend of A, and "aB-2" a man friend of B.

The relationship of the subordinate characters to the protagonist, or to the action, is invariably explained in the text of the Conflicts.

Manipulating Character Symbols

The main Conflict in a plot that is being developed will be the conflict, or situation, under the B Clause of the Masterplot. Subordinate Conflicts, if necessary, will have their character symbols changed, or transposed, to match the symbols of the Conflict whose ramifications are being studied.

In the heart of the text of Conflict 72, you will find a reference: "26a,b, ch A to A-2." Conflict 26a reads: "A and B have never seen each other, etc." If we were using Conflict 26a as explanatory of Conflict 72, our main situation, we would have to change 26a to read: "A-2 and B have never seen each other, etc." Thus the changed symbol, A-2, would come into harmony with the text of Conflict 72. In this illustration, the reference suggests an explanation to account for the fact that A-2 and B, engaged to be married, have never seen each other. This, although important, is a minor point and, in such a case the literal use of the suggestion would be pardonable, although an original interpretation of the specific Conflict is to be preferred.

"Lead-ups" and "Carry-ons"

Reference numbers are prefixed and affixed to the Conflicts. Those prefixed may roughly be designated as "lead-up" Conflicts, in the sense that they lead up to the action of the main Conflict. The reference numbers affixed to the Conflicts may be called "carry-on" suggestions, in the sense that they carry on the action. Reference numbers in the heart of the Conflict text are usually, although not invariably, explanatory suggestions, useful always in studying the plot possibilities of the main Conflict.

Consider, for a moment, Conflict 239. A lead-up to 239 is "291 ch A to A-8." Kindly turn to Conflict 291 and make the change so that 291 shall conform to 239.

Conflict 880a has a lead-up, "840 tr A & A-2." This indicates that characters A and A-2 are to be transposed thus: "A-2 seeks to prevent his friend, A, from committing a reckless act that would have fateful consequences." Then Conflict 880a: "A, by a stratagem of his friend, A-2, is saved from an act of folly, etc."

Turn to Conflict 1052a. Lead-up 1369 suggests that A-4 is to be changed to A-8. Hold the page on which Conflict 1052a appears and turn to Conflict 1369. Read this lead-up, changing the symbol as suggested, in connection with Conflict 1052a.

Now we shall attempt a lead-up combination that is long and has several changes. It will be well to use pencil and paper, or a typewriter, and make a copy of each lead-up reference with the changes as noted. For this illustration we will use the Conflict we have just been considering, 1369. The combination lead-up is long and involved, and refers us first to suggestion 1143b. In 1143b we are to change A to A-8 and B to B-4. Please write out that Conflict with the changes as noted.

Now turn to Conflict 739, the middle term of the suggestion. Write out that Conflict, changing B to B-4.

Now consider conflict 1384, the third suggestion for the combination. B, here, is to be changed to A. Write out this lead-up with the change.

Now kindly turn back to Conflict 1369, our main situation. Arrange the combination Conflicts you have just written down above it in their proper order. All the lead-up Conflicts have been changed to harmonize with 1369:

> "A receives half of an important message, X, and is looking for a stranger, A-4, who has the other half. The message cannot be read until both halves are joined."

Note the difficulty that has to do with the "object X." In our first term of the lead-up combination, X is revealed as a miniature. In our main situation, 1369, we are confronted with a problem; for the miniature is not said to be broken, and the two halves, as the lead-up stands, are already joined.

The constructive imagination of the plottoist could have a piece broken from the miniature, and that fragment in some manner fall into the possession of the stranger, A-4. Or, we might discard the miniature altogether and be even more original in our handling of the situation. Suppose the artist, A-8, has been hired by B-4 to paint two miniatures, one of herself and the other of A-4, her fiancé; and suppose that some of the lines of the concealed "map of great importance" are painted on one miniature, and the rest of the lines on the other. B-4, let us imagine, quarrels with her fiancé. She had intended giving her miniature to A-4, and keeping A-4's miniature for herself; but when they quarrel, B pawns both miniatures; and A-4, discovering what she has done and not knowing that both miniatures "conceal a map of great importance," redeems his own miniature from the pawnbroker.

All lead-ups would carry-on successfully to our main situation. A, with one miniature, would have to secure the other miniature from A-4 before he could have "the map of great importance" complete.

Another interesting study in the interpretation. of suggestion is afforded by Conflict 960a:

> "A is a soldier, eager to fight but is commanded to retreat before a superior force of the enemy * A receives orders from his superiors which he considers discreditable **"

A reference leading up to this Conflict is embodied in suggestion 928b change A to F-A and SN to A:

> "F-A is proud of his son, A* F-A's son, A, dies a shameful, inglorious death, bringing dishonor and sorrow to F-A**"

A carry-on reference is affixed to 960a in a combination: "919c; 928 b ch A to F-A & SN to A." The first part of this suggestion, and the second part with changes as indicated, would read:

> "A, a soldier, is reported a deserter under fire* A, a soldier facing a large force of the enemy, fights against overwhelming odds until he is killed** Then: "F-A is proud of his son, A* F-A's son, A, dies a shameful, inglorious death, bringing dishonor and sorrow to A**"

Here we have a tragic error in which the hero brings sorrow to his father through misinformation given out by the War Office. A would not retreat according to orders; consequently, he is supposed to be a "deserter under fire."

An instructing study in manipulation is offered by this group of Conflicts. Instead of being a soldier, suppose A to be the cashier of a large firm and that he has a large amount of the firm's cash in his possession. The junior partner of the firm employing A is a gambler, and sorely in need of funds. He comes to the office of the firm at night, while A is alone there, working on the books. He orders A to give him a large sum of money from the firm's funds. A refuses, feeling sure that the money wanted is to be used for gambling purposes. Morally, A is in the right; legally, he is in the wrong, for the junior partner has a certain right to the money of the firm. There are hot words, a quarrel, and the junior partner draws a revolver to enforce his demands. In the succeeding tussle, the revolver is discharged, and A is killed. The junior partner takes the cash he needs, places the revolver in A's stiffening fingers and scrawls a note in imitation of A's handwriting to the effect that A is a defaulter, and has taken the easiest way out of his troubles.

This would interpret the suggestion we are studying, removing it from the sphere of military activities and giving, it a setting of civilian life.

Another Interpretation

A-2 is a wealthy man, and the friend of A. A-2 has a fear of burglars that amounts to an obsession. A, surprising a burglar looting his own home, discovers a rare and costly heirloom of A-2's in the possession of the burglar. A does not want A-2 to know he has been robbed, and endeavors to return the heirloom to its owner at night, and by stealth. He uses the robber's mask, effects entrance into A-2's home by the same window the robber had "jimmied" and forced, and then, before he can return the heirloom to the place from which it was taken, he is shot and killed by A-2. To all appearance he is the real robber, for he has the loot in his possession.

Lesson 4 Exercises

1. What was the Masterplot you selected?
2. What Conflict did you exemplify the B Clause of your Masterplot?

3. Interpret originally two suggestions leading up to the selected Conflict.

    a. First Interpretation.

    b. Second Interpretation.

4. Interpret originally two suggestions carrying on and terminating the action suggested by the Conflict selected under the B Clause of your Masterplot.

    a. Second Interpretation.

    b. First Interpretation.

5. Original Conflict References

The fourth lesson concerned itself with the Conflict references. It had previously been observed that of all the hundreds of millions of people in the world, there cannot be found two whose experience with life, and whose spiritual reaction to all the circumstances of environment are identical. The experience of each one of us will vary, widely in most cases and at least in some degree in all cases. This fund of individual knowledge is what we draw upon when we achieve originality in any line of human endeavor. If we are too lazy, or too indifferent, to dig into the soil of our own experience in interpreting suggestion, we become imitators. If we go too exhaustively into the experience of others for what we want, we become plagiarists. The highest honor, and the greatest success of course, comes from turning over the soil in the Field of Originality.

Interpreting Suggestion Originally

"Style," says Buffon, "is the man himself." Dickens has a style of his own, and so has Thackeray. The great Samuel Johnson had a style running to the depth of polysyllables. If he wrote of minnows, it is said that he would have made them talk like whales. "Style is the dress of thoughts," according to Chesterfield. And if we interpret suggestion originally, we should clothe that interpretation in a style of our own, a style that is original with ourselves—natural, easy and anything but "forced." Here again the imagination is to be rightly controlled.

Be Yourself

In writing your plot into story form, interpreting Conflict suggestion originally in narrative prose, be yourself. An individual style in narration will give due attention to restraint. The way an idea is expressed may make or mar the idea itself. We discover our own style by refusing to copy the style of others, by trying to be individual and natural in what we write, never disregarding the limitations or the technicalities of written narrative but adjusting to them our own virgin abilities. The way in which we shall write naturally and most forcefully, usually comes only after much painstaking effort in which we try simply just to be ourselves; in other words, to exercise originality. I write a story in one way, and you will write the same story in another way. The complete story will show a difference of style, a difference of phrasing; but we will be working with our own tools, and the result in each case should be original—and admirable, as everything original is bound to be.

Human Nature

The author of Plotto has selected certain suggestions, and he has called the suggestions Conflicts, and has brought a large number of these Conflicts together in a book. He has gone to *Life* for these Conflicts, and has endeavored to show their possibilities in the form of written narrative. There is nothing original in the Conflicts; for, before ever "Omer smote 'is bloomin' lyre" human nature has been at work throning or dethroning the fortunes of Men. The simplicity of the ancient days has given way to the complexities of modern life, and yet human nature is much the same now that it was in the time of Cain and Abel, or of Helen of Troy. Here and there will be found the refining touch of the centuries, and yet you have only to scratch the veneer of the highest civilization to find the primitive man beneath. Selfishness and greed may be restrained by custom and convention, but when the white-hot emotions boil into action, they overflow convention and we have primitive drama or tragedy, as the case may be.

The References

Reference suggestions prefixed and affixed to the Plotto Conflicts are the random selections of the author of Plotto. They fall in with his ideas as indicated by his experience; and they may not conform to your ideas or agree with your experience. You can take the author of Plotto's suggestions as shown by the references and give them an original interpretation; or, you may search the Conflicts for something that comes nearer harmonizing with your own ideas.

A very successful editor suggested to the author of Plotto that he indicate these supplementary suggestions, primarily for the purpose of familiarizing the student with the Conflicts and with the possibilities of their manipulation. The suggestion was adopted; and so the Conflict references, thousands of them, are given to you in the book as you have it. Bear in mind, however, that they are merely the author's suggestions and that it is your high privilege to discard the suggestions and be original in making your own references. Perhaps it is not only your privilege, but your duty as well as your pleasure. There is a fascination, too, in discarding the Conflict lead-up and carry-on suggestions and in calling upon your imagination to supply you your own. Among its other uses, the Classification of Conflicts by Symbols is designed for this purpose.

Broken Conflicts

"Broken Conflicts" are those Conflicts whose terms are broken, and divided by a star or stars. For instance, Conflict 545 reads as follows: "B's husband, A, fails to return home. A blizzard is raging, and B fears A has suffered a misfortune in the storm* B meets her death while searching vainly in a storm for her husband, A **" This is a broken Conflict, and the whole, or either part of it, may be used. If the first half is to be used, that fact should be expressed by a dash and a star, indicating that the Conflict is to be used up to the first star. If the second half only is to be used, the fact would be indicated by a star, a dash, and a double-star.

Classification by Symbols

All Conflicts are classified in the Classification by symbols. Conflicts not starred are given entire, while broken Conflicts are classified as fragments. The number of the Conflict is appended to each whole or broken Conflict in the Classification, and is thus easily referred to in the Conflict groups. In the Classification by Symbols, also, the Conflicts are brought together under their various subgroup headings, so that a situation in Love's Beginnings, Married Life, Mystery, etc., may be quickly referred to in the sub-group for which a situation is desired. As an added convenience, possible terminal situations are indicated by the numbers of the C Clauses of the Masterplots.

Searching For Original References

Let us experiment with the second half or broken Conflict 690:

> "A, taking a sea voyage, is shipwrecked and cast away on a desert island**"

The first half of the Conflict gives us a motive for A's taking the voyage: "A takes a sea voyage in the hope of recovering his health*" We are assuming that this will not serve, and we are looking for some other motive for the sea voyage on the part of A. We turn to Conflicts in A in the Classification by Symbols. Numerous suggestions are offered for the imagination to work upon. For instance, the A Conflicts in Love's Beginnings has this: "A, who knows nothing of the sciences, pretends to be engaged in scientific research." His pretentions involve him in a sea voyage, and the shipwreck results. Thrown "on his own," and compelled to battle with Nature for his very existence, he develops most unexpectedly the scientific side of his character.

Another suggestion from A Conflicts in Love's Beginnings: "A has taken vows that proscribe the love of woman." Suppose, now that a woman, B, is shipwrecked with A on the desert island, as in Louis Tracy's "The Wings of the Morning." A new situation develops.

A suggestion from Love's Misadventures: "A seeks to escape annoying manifestations of love." He takes a sea voyage to get away from the fair sex. Suppose, as in the previous instance, he is cast away on a desert island with an attractive young woman? Here the imagination will find the beginning of tense drama.

Another suggestion from Love's Misadventures: "A is a crabbed, disagreeable person whose misfortune it is to find no pleasure in life." He takes a sea voyage, is shipwrecked and cast away with, or without, an attractive young woman. In one case, his character will undergo a change through his battling with Nature for existence; in the other case, he falls in love with the young woman, and the necessity of supplying both her wants and his own, will give him an interest in life through love and cause his nature to undergo a change.

A suggestion from A Conflicts in Misfortune: "A, a doctor, is a fugitive from justice." He is escaping from the authorities, and that is his reason for the sea voyage. What follows? Almost anything may follow, for the opportunities for tense drama depend merely upon the circumstances attending the shipwreck. The attractive young woman may also be a castaway, love interest develop, A concealing the fact that he is a fugitive from justice. Suppose the woman, B, A's companion in misfortune, is involved in the transgression our doctor protagonist has committed. Suppose, through B, he discovers his supposed crime was never committed?

Thousands of possibilities will suggest themselves through the scanning of Conflicts in A. When B enters the situation—if she does—the A and B combinations will offer a wealth of suggestions.

A, cast away on his island, will not be limited by the A Conflicts. As a carry-on, glance for a moment at combinations in A and X: "A loses a valuable diamond, X." Or, "A finds a valuable object, X, apparently of great value." Or, "A finds a valuable object, X, between the leaves of a Bible." Or, "A highly prizes an object of mystery, X, carries it about with him and is unaware of the fact that his possession of X is fraught with terrible danger." And so on, *ad infinitum*.

Some of these suggestions would deal with A's experiences after the shipwreck, and while he is on the desert island. In A and A-8 combinations, a lead-up might be used involving the suggestion: "A, against his wish and inclination, has been left a fortune by a deceased relative, A-8." He finances the sea voyage with his inheritance, is cast away, taught a lesson which proves the value of the inheritance, and when he is finally restored to home and friends has undergone a beneficial character transformation.

Any of the Conflict groups involving A might offer a suggestion for the imagination to work upon; or even the B groups with, or without the changing of B to A. Manipulation here is always possible, often with surprising results.

Let us consider Conflict 466a:

> B is married to A, and they have one child, CH* B loves CH, but she does not love A** B loves A-3 and elopes with him leaving her child, CH, with her husband, A***

Looking through the sub-group Transgression, B and A-3, we find this: "B's friend, A-3, mysteriously disappears while in B's company* B is arrested on suspicion of having murdered A-3**" In the combinations, A, B, A-3 and B-3 we find this: "B deserting her husband, A, for A-3, discovers that A-3 is in love with another married woman." In the combination, A, B and CH, we have this suggestion: "B's love for her child, CH, left with her husband, A, when she deserted him, draws her back to CH and A." And so on, again, *ad infinitum*.

Any conflict for which you wish to find a reference of your own will offer a lead-up and carry-on suggestion if you will take the character symbols of the situation you are studying and then look for that combination in the Classification by Symbols. If it should be a long combination, or an unusual combination with only a few Conflicts to choose from, drop one of the lesser symbols and look for the suggestion in the combination that remains. Symbol after symbol may be dropped until only A or B or A and B offer the combination to be studied. Usually the A or B, or the A-B, Conflict combinations will yield suggestions for any of the Conflicts.

By discarding the author's references and searching for your own lead-ups and carry-ons, you will develop your situations in accordance with your own experience and ideas.

Your Short Story

You are to write a short story during this course. In accordance with that idea, you have selected a Masterplot that appealed to you, you have selected a B Clause Conflict to exemplify the Masterplot, and you have used the author's Conflict references to build up the plot, translating the references originally. You are now asked to search out references of your own for leading up to the main Conflict and for carrying the action onward and to a conclusion.

Use the Classification by Symbols, exercise your imagination and draw upon your own experience in interpreting the suggestions. Compare the lead-up and carry-on suggestions of your own selection with those of the author's selection. You will find, undoubtedly, that you can work to better advantage with the lead-up and carry-on suggestions that you have selected for yourself.

If you find it necessary, you may change the C Clause of your Masterplot to harmonize with any finale which appeals to you as better suited to the working out of your plot, or to accord with any fresh idea that may be evolved during this period of plot construction.

Lesson 5 Exercises

1. What was the A Clause of the Masterplot you selected?
2. What original Conflict are you now selecting to illustrate the B Clause?
3. What was your original C Clause?
4. If you have changed the C Clause to harmonize with a new B Clause, please give the New C Clause here:
5. Select originally another B Clause Conflict.

6. Characterization

In commercial affairs, a large organization may have intimate relations with a number of subsidiary organizations. The parent organization, in such a case, may exercise control over the subsidiaries by the devise of having some of the directors of the larger company act also as directors of some of the smaller concerns. The result technically is known as "an interlocking directorate."

If we consider the fundamentals of a story to be theme, plot and characterization, we shall discover that each of the elements interlocks one with the other. This mutual dependence, or interlocking, is brought about in narrative fiction through the interpretation of suggestion.

Characterization Indispensable

Character determines the reaction of a protagonist to the stimuli of environment. A brave man will face a danger from which a cowardly man will flee. Yet here is a generalization capable of many interpretations. The manner in which a brave man will face a danger from which a cowardly man will flee presents a finer problem in characterization. Mass courage, the courage of a Light Brigade charging to death at Balaklava, drops a plummet to the bottom of military duty and leaves nothing more to be said; but the gallant American corporal who, in the World War, captured one machine gun nest after another, typifies the courage and exalts the character of a protagonist who adds resourcefulness to his courage. Bravery and cowardice may have their distinguishing features or peculiarities; and here the larger classifications shade off into innumerable nuances of conduct.

Characterization is an indispensable element in every story. Carried to a point in which it rises paramount to plot and theme, we have the so-called "character" story; with emphasis on the plot, we have the plot story; with emphasis on the theme, the thematic story.

Theme, Plot, Characterization

Technically, there must be a theme, there must be a plot embodying the theme, and there must be characterization exemplifying the plot. The Plotto Masterplot will suggest the theme at the time that it suggests the Masterplot, the Masterplot will suggest the plot, and the plot will suggest the characterization. In Plotto, the technical elements of the story's construction are all interlocked, or dovetailed, one with another.

Situation Decides Characterization

Diderot states that "it is for the situations to decide the characters. The plan of the drama may be drawn, and well drawn, before the poet knows anything of the character he will give his personages." A person's character is best revealed by his acts, rather than through any psychological description by the author. What a man does, is the revelation of what really is. Uriah Heep's "I am so humble," is less eloquent than his shrinking, and the wringing of his hands; and all these are less to the point than his designing, detestable intermeddling.

The situations, then, will decide the characterization. The Masterplots have their veiled character suggestions, and in the Conflicts these suggestions become sufficiently clear for interpretation.

Masterplot Character Suggestion

Glance through the A Clauses of the Masterplots. "A Person in Love," and "A Married Person," are broadly suggestive of status rather than of temperament, but "A Lawless Person," "An Erring Person," "A Benevolent Person," and so on, offer vague suggestions in characterization.

The general suggestions of the B Clauses carry us a step further. "Engaging in a difficult enterprise when promised a reward for high achievement," will suggest a latent courage aroused by the offer of a reward, or high courage girding itself for extraordinary achievement. "Falling in love at a time when certain obligations forbid love," will suggest a character either admirable or despicable.

In the C Clauses also there are these veiled and general character suggestions: "Emerges from a trying ordeal with sorely garnered wisdom," "Meets with an experience whereby an error is corrected," "Discovers the folly of trying to appear otherwise than as one is in reality"—these are all filled with character suggestions.

Conflict Suggestion

However, it remains for the Conflicts to offer more concrete suggestions in character building. Conflict 753, "A, seeking to finance himself, gambles with money not his own—and loses it;" Conflict 544, "B labors under the mistaken belief that her husband, A, receives all the praise for her own kindly acts;" Conflict 196, "A, because of timidity, is unable to ask B's hand in marriage;" and so on. The creative imagination is called upon to furnish character that will meet the conditions of the situation, and all the depths of human nature may be sounded.

You have selected a theme or Masterplot for a short story, and a main Conflict for the story with its lead-up and carry-on suggestions; in short, you have an original plot, and now that plot is to be presented in story form. You are asked, at this time, to resolve your plot into narrative fiction. You will continue to be original in your work. In interpreting actions into character, you will not copy any other author's characterization but you will dig deep into your own knowledge of life and create character in logical explanation of Purpose and Obstacle. Obstacle itself will suggest characterization in the matter of the antagonist, and every angle of the situation will afford character clues for the subordinate actors in the drama.

Along this line of Conflict character suggestion, let us for a moment study Conflict 92:

> B is in love with A, who has been arrested on a criminal charge by A-6* B, in order to help her lover, A, escape from A-6, the officer who has arrested him, makes love to A-6**

What would you consider to be the character of B in this situation? There are various interpretations. The highest interpretation would picture B as a woman of Puritanical principles who, rendered desperate by the plight of the man she loves, turns her back on her principles and, in a spirit of self-sacrifice, plays the role of a wanton. A-6, the antagonist, would be a man of loose character to whom the beauty of A's sweetheart, B, carries an irresistible appeal. A, high-souled victim of circumstantial evidence, would watch the coquetry of B and perhaps misinterpret its cause.

On the other hand, a second interpretation would picture A and B as criminals, with A counseling B in her drab pretentions; and A-6 would be of wavering character, or consecrated to professional duty, as the plot might indicate.

Again, B might be high principled. Persuaded by A to flirt with A-6, B might for the first time secure light on the despicable character of A, and thus alter the whole course of her future. Here the character trend of all factors in the situation would depend upon the Clauses of the Masterplot.

Inventing character as a logical explanation of Conflict circumstances, develops the powers of characterization and makes for facility in original interpretation.

Style

The phrasing of a narrative story is a matter of style, of your own style and an expression of your own individuality if these lessons have not been in vain. Let your style be one of the utmost simplicity, by all means—a style of Anglo-Saxon words rather than of their Latinized synonyms or near-synonyms. There will be variations of individual style exacted by the theme. Humor will decide one variation, and pathos another; satire will lend the phrasing another note, if you care to write a story in that pitch; but each and all, let it be remembered, are variations of your own style.

If the plot has been properly constructed, the technical requirements of introduction, ascending action, crisis and dénouement have all been taken care of. It remains for style to give no more place to action than action demands. A short story is the most difficult piece of work in all fiction. Nothing may be left out that will help to convey the single dominant impression to the reader's mind, and nothing may be added that will blur or confuse that impression. Think of the reader when you are writing your story. All your ideas are clear to you, but will they be clear to him? Apart from plain lucidity, there is a strength and manliness in simplicity that rarely fails to impress the reader.

The Beginning

At the very beginning of your story there are pitfalls to be avoided. Interest your reader at the start, with the first sentence if possible, certainly with the first paragraph. In Donn

Byrne's book, "Changeling and Other Short Stories," there is not one that begins with dialogue. But Byrne's openings are descriptive in a way that grips and holds the attention of the reader. Note these: "Because of his perfect, or nearly perfect, English there were many who believed that Li Sin was merely masquerading as a Chinaman." "Very much as though he were entering a disreputable place, Matthew Kerrigan, etc." "To him the whole conversation, the whole setting, the whole event, were unreal as ghosts are unreal," etc.

Galsworthy is equally subtle in his mastery of the short story as a whole and in its beginnings. "Its psychic origin, like that of most human loves and hates, were obscure." "The affectionate if rather mocking friend who had said of Charles Grantor: "He isn't a man, he's an edifice," etc."

At the first swing of your driver get the ball into the fairway of your story. Begin with the story, and not with a lot of circumlocution leading up to the beginning. A short story has no words to waste.

Lesson 6 Exercises

1. Characterize briefly "An Erring Person."
2. Characterize briefly "Being impelled by an unusual motive to engage in crafty enterprise."
   a. What was the "unusual motive?"
   b. What was "the crafty enterprise?"
   c. What character was needed for motive and enterprise?
3. How was character of protagonist changed in C Clause (14): "Achieves a complete and permanent character transformation?"
4. Write a short story of not more than 5,000 words around the Masterplot, Conflicts and original references already selected.

7. Individualizing Plotto

This is to be the last lesson; and in this, the final lesson, there are several important matters to be discussed.

First, there is one very helpful practice in connection with the Plotto Method, and it has to do with what may be called "individualizing Plotto." You individualize Plotto, of course, when you interpret Conflict suggestions originally, but it is possible to go a step further.

Indexing Story Material

Every writer collects material which he thinks may be of use in his work. The material may be in the form of newspaper clippings, or of notes jotted down in a commonplace book and having possibilities as story material. As the years pass, these gathered suggestions become so voluminous as to lead to confusion and so defeat the purpose for which they were collected. It is possible, through Plotto, to make all this store of suggestions instantly available.

File the material away alphabetically in a box file. Reduce the major situations to Conflict under the proper Clause of the Masterplot and in the group and sub-group to which it belongs; then, in your Plotto, make a notation on the margin opposite the Conflict which the added situation most closely approximates, and under the B Clause of the proper sub-group. By indexing in this manner, all your gathered situations may be referred to instantly.

Plotto as a Personal Aid

There is another, and perhaps a vastly more important matter, which may be considered here under the caption, "Individualizing Plotto." In all the preceding lessons we have dealt with Plotto as an aid in story writing; but it may be made helpful in other ways, helpful to you personally in a manner that has nothing to do with Masterplots, plots and characterization for written narrative.

Remember that:

Imagination, Rightfully Controlled, is the Greatest Force in the World.

"Imagination," as Pascal tells us, "disposes of everything; it creates beauty, justice and happiness, which is everything in this world." With Plotto it is possible to develop, and to achieve right control of, the imagination.

The Man of Vision

If you were never to write a story, with Plotto as your handbook, it is within your power to develop your originality and "create beauty, justice and happiness" in whatever sphere of life you choose to occupy. Whether a man shall sell mousetraps or life insurance, stories or dry goods, he will find in his imagination a power which, furthering his originality, will bring to him pleasure and profit such as he has never known before. As John Abercrombie writes: "The sound and proper exercise of the imagination may be made to contribute to the cultivation of all that is virtuous and estimable in the human character."

The man of "vision" is the man of imagination rightfully controlled. The glittering opportunities this world has to offer are for such men alone. An imagination of ever-growing power, rightly controlled in the direction of a certain goal, made the ancient Alexander "Great," made Socrates, Aristotle, Bergson and James the philosophers they became, made Washington "the father of his country," Abraham Lincoln the dominant figure of his period, and Theodore Roosevelt the national apostle of the strenuous life. It is this type of imagination that gave us our Thomas Edison, our Henry Ford, and our famous Lindbergh; and it gave us, of course, our William Dean Howells, Nathaniel Hawthorne, Wilbur Steele, Fanny Hurst and Mary Roberts Rhinehart.

Coach the Imagination Constantly

Imagination rightly controlled gives us notable character; wrongly controlled, it gives us notorious characters. As the author of Plotto believes, the Plotto Method is ideal and at its best when, through the original interpretation of Conflict suggestions, it helps the imagination to grow systematically and in the right direction. Coach the imagination constantly with the Conflict suggestions, not alone when engaged in your story work, but also in your leisure moments; as your imagination grows and becomes trained to keep the path to its proper goal, your capabilities will grow with it. A ready imagination, directed toward higher ends, brings the highest realizations, a glorious measure of happiness and success—possible with originality and impossible without it.

Personal Interpretation of Conflict Suggestion

In story writing we are dealing with aspects of *Life;* story writing apart, in any field of endeavor Conflict suggestions may be interpreted in terms personal to yourself, and will be found wonderfully helpful in meeting your problems.

Since the Conflict suggestions hold the mirror up to life, it is necessary that they should reflect the admirable no less than the contemptible, for these traits are a part of human nature and will find their way into stories. The Conflicts must be all-embracing, and run the gamut of human existence. The nobler Conflicts studied with a personal application will ennoble the character.

There will be found a comforting, an instructive and a healing quality in such a study. Many of the Conflicts in all groups, but especially in the subgroups Idealism, Helpfulness and Deliverance, are potent for good if the imagination is allowed to play about them originally.

In the suggestion of Conflict 900 we see how imagination, not rightly controlled, may plunge a person into misfortune. The self-sacrifice of Conflict 906, the lofty lesson of Conflict 907, both offer suggestions around which the fancy may play with the most happy results. It is little short of amazing what wrong imagination will do to us, and what right imagination will do for us.

If cast down and dispirited by the evil of the world, study Conflict 939; if the evils consequent upon the possession of great wealth has saddened and bewildered you, give your fancy rein with Conflict 940; if you are in pecuniary distress, meditate upon Conflicts 941 and 942; if a friend proves disloyal, range the high fields of idealism with Conflicts 943b and 944; if discontented, muse upon the suggestions of Conflicts 950 and 954; if suffering injustice, spend a few minutes with Conflict 919a; if you have committed a wrong and are troubled by conscience, walk with the protagonist of Conflict 918a; if you are in sorrow, consider Conflict 918b; if your pride is excessive, a study of Conflict 920 should humble it; and if your ideals are low, consider that fact in the right of Conflict 922b, supplemented with Conflict 922a.

Imagination Palliative of Evil

Wrong moods are the consequence of imagination improperly developed; and for every wrong mood there is a corrective suggestion in right control of "the greatest force in the world." Not only is the imagination palliative or evil, it is positive in its influence upon success. The suggestions of the nobler Conflicts have tremendous power for you, for me, for every one who will let the imagination work with them. We are original in our errors of omission and commission, so let us be original in the methods of their correction. Purpose, here, will surely overcome Obstacle if the imagination is rightly controlled. And there will be no purpose unless there is an emotion, and earnest desire, as the source of it.

Possibility of Misunderstanding

To the author of Plotto a mere reading of the book has proved the difficulty of bringing home to the mind the vast possibilities embraced in the Conflicts. To combat a misunderstanding of the Method, and to inculcate practically the Method's ideals, this course of lessons has been devised.

Plotto Truth

For more than forty years the author of Plotto has been writing and selling fiction stories; and out of this long experience he earnestly believes that here in Plotto is *Truth,* and a Method of Originality as firmly founded as human nature itself. The author of Plotto has given five years to the preparation of this work. He knows it is imperfect, and that it would still be imperfect if he had spent a whole lifetime in its preparation. But he has proved that it is practical.

How the Work was Devised

The author began his work by devising the Masterplot Chart; and, because of his long experience in story writing, he found the Masterplots sufficient for his purposes of plot suggestion. But when these Masterplots were submitted to other writers, there was the objection that they were not concrete enough in their suggestions. To make the Masterplot supply his need, the Conflicts to exemplify them were devised—calling for the most intense application over a period of years. The author of Plotto has made use of the Conflict suggestions in his own work, and is using them now, always with the utmost success. In fact, he has been told by the publisher who has used most of his output of fiction for forty years, that, contrary to the rule, his "work grows better as his years increase." And that is because Plotto, a Method that has done and is doing its best with its author's plodding talent. Having himself demonstrated the practicability of the Method, the author passes it on to others with confidence that, if used in an original way, the ideal way, it will easily demonstrate its value.

Possibilities in Originality

A very great and successful author told the author of Plotto that "he could never use it in his work." He perhaps had the idea which a publisher in London, England, when he remarked: "Plotto will be condemned publicly—and probably used privately." But the American author and the London publisher spoke hastily; they had not penetrated to the real nature of this work by scanning its possibilities in originality. Even the accomplished author, the author who has "arrived," will find in the Plotto Conflicts the fire needed.

The End

Also from Norton Creek Press

*Plotto: The Classic Plot Suggestion Tool
for Writers of Creative Fiction*
William Wallace Cook

The Fiction Factory
William Wallace Cook

Printed by Amazon Italia Logistica S.r.l.
Torrazza Piemonte (TO), Italy